Rainy Day Play

EXPLORE
CREATE
DISCOVER
PRETEND

NANCY F. CASTALDO

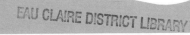

CHICAGO
REVIEW
PRESS

Library of Congress Cataloging-in-Publication Data

Is available from the Library of Congress.

Cover design and illustration: Fran Lee

Interior design and illustration: Sheree Boyd

© 1997, 2005 by Nancy F. Castaldo

Illustrations © Sheree Boyd
Published by Chicago Review Press, Incorporated

814 North Franklin Street

Chicago, Illinois 60610

ISBN 1-55652-563-X

Printed in the United States of America

5 4 3 2 1

Contents

For the little ones, Jared, Jason, Jenny, Gavin,
Erin, Caroline, and Katherine

Bright Thoughts About Rainy Days

A Note to Grown-Ups

Rainy days present challenges to adults with children in their care, whether parent, grandparent, caregiver, or teacher. But it can be a positive challenge, as rainy days create wonderful opportunities for precious, shared time.

We all have days when we have to pop a video in the VCR. But when time is available and the videos have gotten old, consider reading a book or making up stories together instead. If you were thinking of setting out coloring books and crayons, turn to some of the art activities in the index (pages 141-142), which are almost as easy and mess-free. And don't overlook the fact that what is tedious to you may be fascinating and valuable to preschoolers. Give them a chance to dust, stack some books, or put away the groceries. They'll love doing it and will be very proud, knowing that you gave them such a big responsibility.

The experiences suggested within may take as little or as much time as you would like. They are meant to provide a stepping stone to further ideas and fun that you will discover together. Each activity is multifaceted, giving preschoolers experience with such things as numbers, letters, imagination, and directions. At this age, the process of creative thinking is as valuable as the outcome. Everyone comes out a winner!

Who knows? Maybe rainy days will become favorite days just because they force us to slow down a bit, so we can share time and space and giggles and learning with little ones.

COZY CORNER PLAY

When the rain is falling all around and your house is dry and safe, that is the time to nestle down and play and play and play!

If I Were

If you could be anything, what would you be? A giant-sized animal? Something that flies like an airplane? A truck driver? A tiny ant? Here's a chance to imagine being anything you like.

HERE'S WHAT YOU NEED

Open space

At least one other person

HERE'S WHAT YOU DO

1 Think of something or someone you would like to be—like an animal or a tree, or a mail delivery person or a ballet dancer.

2 Now, without speaking, act out something that person or thing would do. For instance, "If I were a bird, I would fly through the sky." Let everyone guess what or who you are.

3 Take turns acting out and guessing what you are.

LET IT POUR!

✳ How does it feel to be someone or something else? Can you imagine a whole day as that person or thing? Try being it for five whole minutes.

✳ Play Nursery Rhyme Charades. Take turns acting out your favorite nursery rhymes or storybook characters.

✳ Imagine that you are an animal outside in the rain. Do you like the rain or do you want to find protection?

Cozy Corner

Cinderella's cozy corner was near her fireplace. There she could imagine being in faraway places, read her favorite stories, or just curl up and listen to the raindrops falling on the roof. Cozy corners sure are special places!

HERE'S WHAT YOU NEED

Pillows and blanket

Books

Crayons and paper

Games

HERE'S WHAT YOU DO

1 Find a cozy place in your house—in a corner, under a table, or wherever. Place your blanket on the floor and pile on some pillows and maybe a stuffed animal or small toy car, too.

2 Sit in your cozy spot; listen to the rain. Is the rain coming down very **fast** and **hard**? Is it raining gently, with a comforting tap, tap, tap?

3 Enjoy your cozy corner. Color, play a game, look at a book, or have a nice warm cup of cocoa.

LET IT POUR!

❋ Listen to *Weather: Poems for All Seasons* by Lee Bennett Hopkins for some great poems about weather.

❋ Talk about what makes you feel safe and cozy. When don't you feel safe and cozy?

❋ Try singing "Rain, Rain, Go Away" or "It's Raining, It's Pouring" as a round, while you listen to the rain fall outside.

11

Marathon Book Festival

Celebrate books with your own marathon book festival! Invite a friend to join in the fun.

HERE'S WHAT YOU NEED

A variety of books

HERE'S WHAT YOU DO

1 Pick a subject to be the focus of your book festival. This is called the **theme**. You might pick trucks, dinosaurs, rabbits, or the seashore.

2 Search your shelves and books for stories and poems about your theme. Read them together with a grown-up.

3 Talk about the stories you read together and why you like some stories and maybe don't like other stories.

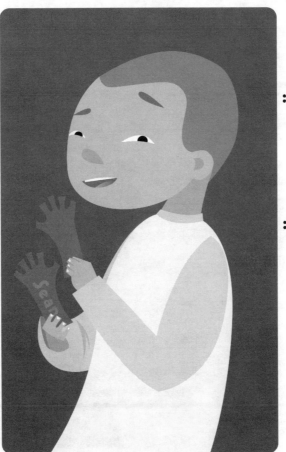

LET IT POUR!

❋ Tell your own story to a grown-up who can write it down. Leave room on each page for your own illustrations.

❋ On your next visit to the library, pick out books on a different theme. Try finding books about bears, dancing, food, or bugs!

❋ Place your hand flat on a piece of construction paper and trace around it. Cut out the hand shape and write your name on it for a handmade bookmark.

13

Rhyme Rap

Rhyming words, such as cat *and* hat *or* three *and* me, *sound alike. It's fun to rhyme—if you've got the time!*

HERE'S WHAT YOU NEED

Poetry books

HERE'S WHAT YOU DO

1 Read different kinds of poetry with a grown-up. Some poems rhyme and some poems don't. It is fun to listen for the rhyming words.

2 Say a word, any word (*cat* is a good one to start with). How many words can you think of that rhyme with your word?

LET IT POUR!

* Listen to some of these great poetry books: *Sing a Song of Popcorn* selected by Beatrice De Regniers, *Chicka Chicka Boom Boom* by Bill Martin Jr., and *A Child's Garden of Verse* by Robert Louis Stevenson. Pick out your favorite poem.

* Start a rhyme journal. Cut out or draw pictures of rhyming words like a *mouse* and a *house*.

* Rhymes can lead to some very silly sayings. Make up a silly saying with rhyming words.

* Play a rhyming game. One person says a word like *red* and the other says a rhyme like "I sat on my bed." Listen to *What Rhymes with Eel?* by Harriet Ziefert.

LIGHTNING BOLT!

* When we use a word to imitate a sound like *buzz, hiss,* or *vroom! vroom!*, we are using words to bring a sound to life. In poetry this is called **onomatopoeia**. What other words copy the sound something makes?

Moo, Baa, La La La

Children in England play a game very similar to this. Do you think a cow says moo in far-off countries like England?

HERE'S WHAT YOU DO

1. Everybody picks an animal with a special animal noise like *moo* or *neigh*.

2. A grown-up makes up a story including all of the animals. When you hear the name of your animal, make that animal's sound.

3. If the storyteller says "zoo," then all the animals make their noises together.

HERE'S WHAT YOU NEED

Good, strong voices!
(the more the merrier)

wu wu wu

qua qua

mo mo

LET IT POUR!

❋ Talk about animal sounds in other countries. If you know someone who speaks another language, ask how to describe the sound a cow or a dog makes. Is it *moo* or *bow wow*?

❋ Look in a book or in old *National Geographic* magazines for pictures of animals in other parts of the world. Do they look the **same** or **different** from the animals you see outdoors?

❋ In North America, many people have dogs, cats, birds, or fish for pets. Ask someone who has lived or traveled in another part of the world what kinds of pets children have there.

miyau miyau

piyo piyo

bu bu

LIGHTNING BOLT!

❋ In the United States, cows seem to say *moo moo*, ducks say *quack quack*, and pigs say *oink oink*.

❋ Children in Japan describe animal sounds differently. There, ducks say *ga ga*, cows say *mo mo*, chickens say *piyo piyo*, and pigs say *bu bu*.

❋ In Rwanda, dogs say *wu, wu, wu* and roosters say guglug, *guglug, guglug*. African cats say *miyau, miyau* and cows say *baaah, baaah, baaah*.

❋ In Italy, ducks say *qua, qua*.

❋ German roosters don't say *cocka-doodle-doo*; they say *kikiriki*.

❋ Now here is a very tricky question: Do you think the animals make different sounds or do people just describe them differently depending on where they grow up?

17

Going Batty!

If you go outdoors on a summer's night, you'll probably see some bats overhead, as they hunt for mosquitoes. Don't be afraid; bats rarely go near people. They're too busy finding their dinner!

cut out two black circles

zigzag cut one circle in half

glue half circle wings on each side of bat body

punch hole in top and attach yarn to hang

HERE'S WHAT YOU NEED

Black construction paper

Safety scissors

White craft glue

Hole punch

Yarn

HERE'S WHAT YOU DO

1 Ask a grown-up to help you cut two circles of the same size out of the construction paper.

2 Cut one circle in half, using a zigzag cut.

3 To create bat wings, glue a half circle to each side of the whole circle. Attach a piece of yarn to hang it up.

LET IT POUR!

* Some people think that bats are a kind of bird, but they are not. What is the **same** about a bird and a bat, and what is **different**? Listen to *Stellaluna* by Janell Cannon to hear about a fruit bat that lived with a bird family.

* Learn all about bats in *Zipping, Zapping, Zooming Bats* by Ann Earle.

LIGHTNING BOLT!

* Bats hunt for their food using a system almost like radar. They send out sound wave signals and then, depending on how the sound waves bounce back, they can tell how near something is. This system is so finely tuned that bats can find flying mosquitoes. In fact, each bat can eat about 600 mosquitoes in an hour! Now, that's a bat with a big appetite.

sound wave signals

echoes bounce back

My Special Letters

Words come alive, just wait and see. There's so much more than A, B, C.

HERE'S WHAT YOU DO

1 Your initials are the first letter of your first, last, and middle names. If your name is **J**ohn **S**tanley **G**reene, your initials are **JSG**.

2 Ask a grown-up to help you write down and sound out your initials.

3 Starting with the letter of your first name, cut out pictures that begin with that letter's sound. Draw the letter nice and big on a piece of construction paper and then glue all the pictures around the letter.

4 Do the same thing for each of your initials. Now you have a book of your initial sounds.

5 To make a cover, trace your initials on a piece of paper and glue your photograph on it.

PAGES
Glue one initial then glue pictures that have the initial's sound

Punch holes in cover and pages then tie with yarn

COVER
Glue on initials and picture of yourself

6 Punch holes in your pages and tie them together with a piece of yarn.

LET IT POUR!

❋ If you can spell your first name, make a book with each letter's alphabet sounds.

❋ Ask a friend or two to help you make an alphabet book. Each of you take certain letters of the alphabet and cut out pictures with those letters' sounds.

❋ Look at other alphabet picture books. *Pigs from A to Z* by Arthur Geisert and *Amazon Alphabet* by Tanis Jordan are just two that are wonderful to read together.

OUTDOOR RAINY DAY FUN!

All rainy days don't have to be inside days. On days that are warm with a light rain falling, you might be able to venture outdoors for a while. Oh, what fun it will be!

Puddle Walk

A gentle rain is falling and you are dressed in your boots and your raincoat. (Or maybe it is very warm and you can go outside in your bathing suit!) Here's some fun for days that are wet and drippy.

HERE'S WHAT YOU NEED

Appropriate clothing

Hand lens

HERE'S WHAT YOU DO

1. Dress according to the outdoor temperature and then take a rainy day walk around your yard or down the street with a grown-up.

2. There may not be many people outdoors, but there will be a lot of critters out and about. Look for **worms** that come out of the ground during the rain and end up on walkways. Look for spider webs covered with raindrops. Are you surprised that the rain hasn't washed away the webs?

3. With your hand lens, examine raindrops that sit like tiny bubbles on leaves or railings.

4. How does the rain feel? Stick out your tongue and catch a raindrop. Touch leaves, soil, and rocks. Feel the squishy ground beneath your feet.

LET IT POUR!

* Talk about the difference between summer rainy days and fall rainy days.

* Play I Spy in the rain. Each player picks something for the other player to find. For example, "I spy a leaping frog" or "I spy a slippery leaf."

* Look for rainy day critters like snails, frogs, toads, and salamanders. Then go indoors, dry off, and listen to *The Salamander Room* by Anne Mazer.

* Look for rainbows just as the sun begins to burst forth.

Drip Drop

Drip drop, pitter patter, ping pong! The sounds of raindrops have many voices. Let's listen together.

HERE'S WHAT YOU NEED

Rain gear
Variety of metal, glass, and plastic containers

HERE'S WHAT YOU DO

1 Dress according to the weather. Place the containers upside down, one at a time in the rain. What sound does the rain make as it falls on each container?

2 Add groups of containers to create your own rainy day chorus. Which containers make the loudest sound?

3 Turn some containers right side up. Does the sound change as the containers begin to fill up with water?

4 Place some of the containers under a heavier drip, like rain dripping off the edge of the roof. Is the sound different?

LET IT POUR!

✳ Use the containers to measure the rainfall. Which containers fill up more quickly? Use a ruler to measure how much rain has fallen into each container. Why do the amounts differ?

✳ Listen to the weather report to find out how much rain actually fell for that day. Which container measured the closest amount?

✳ Listen to *Cloudy with a Chance of Meatballs* and *Return to Chewandswallow* by Judi Barrett. Then pretend you are collecting food instead of raindrops in your containers.

27

Play Leap Frog

Bend those legs and jump like a frog! How high can you jump? Leap Frog is so much fun.

HERE'S WHAT YOU NEED

Open space on soft ground

HERE'S WHAT YOU DO

1. Find an open area on the grass. Have one player squat down.

2. With your hands on the player's back, leap over him or her.

3. Set up a long line of jumpers. The person on the end jumps over everyone else and finishes in a squatting position in the front.

4. Make frog noises as you play. Ribbit! Ribbit!

LET IT POUR!

* With a grown-up, take a walk around a pond to watch some real frogs leaping.

* To meet some wonderful frogs and toads, listen to Arnold Lobel's frog and toad stories.

* Can't go outdoors today? Play Leap Frog inside and leap from room to room.

LIGHTNING BOLT!

* Did you know that frogs and toads are not the same? Almost all toads have bumpy, warty, brown or gray skin; frogs are known to have smooth, green skin. You will see more frogs near the water. Toads spend most of their time on land. You might even find one living in a flowerpot.

* Toads generally do more hopping and are sometimes called hop-toads. Frogs are mostly leapers. Try hopping like a toad and leaping like a frog!

Splish! Splash! Give a Plant a Bath!

A gentle rainfall is the perfect time to give your indoor houseplants a much-needed shower. They'll thank you for it by growing healthier.

HERE'S WHAT YOU NEED

Indoor plants

Cotton swabs

A gentle rain

HERE'S WHAT YOU DO

1   Place your plants outside.

2   Let your plants enjoy the light rain shower. Use cotton swabs to clean leaves and get rid of any mites (they look like specks of cotton).

3   After about half an hour, shake your plants slightly to remove extra water before taking them back inside.

4   Place your plants in a bathtub or sink or on a counter to let them dry before setting them back in their original places in the house.

5   Don't they look refreshed?

LET IT POUR!

* Watch the water fall on the leaves. Does the water sit on the leaf or roll right off?

* Clean off any dead leaves from your plants.

* Help a grown-up repot a plant that has grown too big for its pot.

* Many leaves are **dark green**, but some are **bright green, red, purple,** and even **striped** in two colors. What colors are your plants' leaves?

LIGHTNING BOLT!

* Do you know why it is so important to give your plants a shower? Plants actually breathe through their leaves—not by taking deep breaths like you and me, but by absorbing fresh air through their leaves. So if the leaves are dusty, it is harder for them to breathe.

Puddle Power

Jump in a puddle and splash about. Where will it go? Let's find out.

HERE'S WHAT YOU NEED

Chalk

Puddles

HERE'S WHAT YOU DO

1 After a rainfall, take a walk outside to find puddles. Draw a chalk outline around each puddle (or outline it with a mark drawn with a stick in the soil).

2 What sounds do you hear after the rain stops? Do you hear water dripping? Birds singing? It is a wonderful time to be outdoors.

3 Now go back to your puddle and watch what happens to it as the ground begins to dry. How did your puddle change?

LET IT POUR!

✳ Watch birds enjoy the puddles after a rainfall. What are they doing?

✳ Try skipping flat stones on a big puddle.

✳ Make a paper toy boat and float it on a puddle after the rain stops. Or float a leaf on the puddle.

LIGHTNING BOLT!

✳ Where do you think the water in the puddle went? If you guessed that it dried up, you are partially correct. The water did dry up, but it didn't disappear. It actually was heated up by the sun and, in drops even smaller than raindrops, it floated back up toward the sky again. This is called **evaporation**. Now, do you want to know something really curious? When it rains somewhere else, some of those same drops of water that evaporated will fall back to earth again, perhaps into a new puddle.

Mudpies, Weeds, and Seeds

Some people say you shouldn't garden in the rain, but for little hands there is no better time because the earth is warm and moist.

HERE'S WHAT YOU NEED

Old clothes

Gloves

1 Wear appropriate clothing for a muddy day. The ground is nice and soft when it rains, making it a great time to help a grown-up pull up the weeds. Gently pull from just above the ground so the roots come out, too.

2 Take a close look at the roots, stem, and flower (if there is one). Notice if the root is long and thick, or if there are a lot of tiny roots.

3 Here's a curious question: is there a difference between a weed and a flower that is left to grow in the garden?

4 When a soft rain is falling, it's also a great time for planting. The ground is soft and can easily be dug to make room for seeds or new plants. And you won't have to water!

LET IT POUR!

✳ Besides weeds, there are other pests that people try to keep out of gardens. Listen to *The Tale of Peter Rabbit* to learn about one such critter who couldn't stay out of a vegetable garden.

✳ What's a summer rain without mudpies? Make mudpies with the wet soil. Decorate them with leaves, sticks, pebbles, and flowers. Set them out to bake when the sun comes out.

ART SMART!

Some people think of rainy days as dull, gray days. It doesn't have to be that way, of course. You can fill your rainy days with lots of bright colors and fun things to do!

Who Needs a Brush?

You don't need a paintbrush to paint a great picture. In fact, sometimes it's even more fun without one!

HERE'S WHAT YOU NEED

Newspaper

Container of water

Egg carton

Washable tempera paint

Finger paints

paper

All sorts of possible painting tools

HERE'S WHAT YOU DO

1 Collect old toothbrushes, toothpicks, feathers, straws, and other things that might make unusual painting tools. Cover the table with newspaper.

2 Pour the paint into the egg carton sections.

3 Experiment with your tools and your paint. Do you get lots of thin lines with a toothbrush and a big fat line with a cotton swab? What tool can you use to paint animal fur?

4 Paint your own masterpiece!

LET IT POUR!

✳ Talk about the appearance of different **textures** you created with your painting tools. Which ones look **smooth? Rough?**

✳ Make mystery rubbings of objects around your house or classroom with crayons. What surface works best for your rubbings—rough or smooth? Ask someone to guess where the rubbing came from.

smooth

rough

LIGHTNING BOLT!

✳ Artists apply their paints using many different tools, just as you did. They also create different effects by using various kinds of paint, like watercolors or oils, and by using different kinds of paper, like rice paper or canvas. Do you have a favorite way to draw using crayons, markers, or paints?

Stained-Glass Raindrops

While you are watching the falling rain, you can make your own raindrops to hang on your windows.

HERE'S WHAT YOU NEED

Sheet of clear plastic

Safety scissors

Marker

Assorted colors of beeswax

HERE'S WHAT YOU DO

1 Ask a grown-up to cut the plastic sheet in half. Then draw the shape of a raindrop on one half of the plastic. Layer the two plastic halves and cut out two identical raindrops.

2 Lay one raindrop flat on a table. Take a pea-sized or smaller piece of the beeswax in your hand. Roll it around, warming it up in your hands, softening it.

3 Press the beeswax onto the plastic. Continue adding beeswax pieces until the entire raindrop is filled with multi-colored flat pieces of wax.

4 Place the other plastic raindrop on top of the wax. Press the sheet onto the wax, sticking the two sides together.

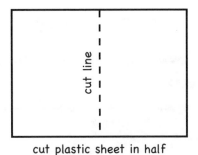

cut line

cut plastic sheet in half

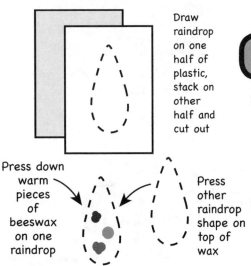

Draw raindrop on one half of plastic, stack on other half and cut out

Press down warm pieces of beeswax on one raindrop

Press other raindrop shape on top of wax

5 Ask a grown-up to punch a hole in the top of the raindrop so you can hang it from a window. Now even on the rainiest day you can still have some color shining in your window!

LET IT POUR!

❋ Use the plastic sheets and beeswax to make a variety of stained-glass shapes. Try hearts and diamonds—even your initials!

❋ The next time you are in the grocery store, look for honey still in a honeycomb. If you can buy it, take it home, look at how the bees made it, and then eat some honey.

Almost Batik

Sometimes making art means using unusual methods. Here's something very unusual that turns out very nicely.

HERE'S WHAT YOU NEED

Crayons

White paper

Water

Newspaper

Watercolors

Paintbrush

HERE'S WHAT YOU DO

1 Draw a picture with crayons on white paper.

2 Place your picture in water. After a few minutes, gently remove the paper and crumble it into a ball.

3 Then open up the paper and place it flat on the newspaper. Paint all over the entire sheet with your watercolor paint. Dip the picture back into the water for a quick minute.

4 Remove the picture and place it flat to dry on the newspaper.

LET IT POUR!

✳ What part of the directions for Almost Batik seemed unusual to you?

✳ Create an ocean picture by drawing fish and other marine critters with your crayons. Paint over the entire picture with watered-down blue watercolor paint. See how the waxy crayons keep the blue paint off.

LIGHTNING BOLT!

✳ Batik is an art originally used by the people of Java to decorate cloth. The artist uses hot wax to make a design, like the crayon does in the activity. The cloth is then dyed. The dye clings to the unwaxed areas of the cloth, leaving the waxed areas white. Later, the wax is scraped or boiled off the fabric and the design appears.

Dinner Is Served!

Set yourself up for some fun—and get ready to set the dinner table, too!
You can make some festive woven place mats for a dinnertime surprise!

HERE'S WHAT YOU NEED

Construction paper

Safety scissors

Stapler or glue

HERE'S WHAT YOU DO

1 Ask a grown-up to help you cut the construction paper length-wise into strips for weaving.

2 Arrange four strips into a square border for your place mat. Ask a grown-up to glue the corners forming a square.

3 Next, glue or staple strips across the square to create a base for your weaving.

4 Weave strips of construction paper over and under the base strips. Finish by gluing or stapling down the ends.

LET IT POUR!

✻ Set the table with your colorful place mats. Add forks to the left of the plate and spoons to the right.

✻ Make a centerpiece for the table. It could be a small teddy bear, some wildflowers, or an arrangement of fresh fruits and vegetables.

LIGHTNING BOLT!

✻ People in other parts of the world have different dining traditions and eating utensils. Learn how people in other countries set their tables for dinner. Try eating with chopsticks as some Asian people do, or set dinner on a coffee table and sit on pillows in the style of Japanese dining.

sushi!

chopsticks!

Wacky Hats

It many not be the right hat for a walk in the rain, but this will surely turn heads when you wear it!

1 Ask a grown-up to cut about 2 to 3 inches (5 cm—7.5 cm) straight across the bottom of the plate. Next, cut out the center.

2 Try on the plate for size. It should fit like a headband.

3 Cut out shapes from construction paper and glue them to the plate.

4 Decorate the hat with streamers, glitter, flowers—or whatever—to make the wackiest hat ever.

cut

cut

LET IT POUR!

✳ Put your Wacky Hat on and listen to *Jennie's Hat* by Ezra Jack Keats, *Caps for Sale* by Esphyr Slobodkina, and Dr. Seuss's *The Cat in the Hat.*

✳ Take an old hat and dress it up with feathers, silk flowers, ribbons, and any other decorations.

✳ Make a "Just-for-You" gift hat with special decorations like golf tees for someone who golfs or small wooden blocks and small toys for a friend.

✳ Cheer up someone at school or at home. Make a courtly crown out of construction paper, decorate it with glitter and sequins, and name that person king or queen for the day.

Cereal Mosaic

You don't need much to create this masterpiece—just look at your cereal bowl and let your imagination soar!

HERE'S WHAT YOU NEED

Craft glue

Construction paper

Cardboard

Toothpick or cotton swab

Cereal

HERE'S WHAT YOU DO

1 Spread some craft glue on the back of the construction paper and glue it to the cardboard. Let dry.

2 Dip the toothpick into the glue. Using the toothpick like a pencil, draw a shape, design, or letter on the paper. Fill in the shape with glue, too, if you choose.

3 Place cereal pieces close together, wherever you have glue. Allow the mosaic to dry.

LET IT POUR!

✳ While you are making your mosaic, name all the kinds of cereal you can think of. Then, name only the ones you like. How many do you like?

✳ What other breakfast foods can you name? Talk about why breakfast is important.

✳ Use dried beans, rice, and macaroni to make another mosaic picture.

Crazy Critter

Have fun sculpting your own Crazy Critter!

Egg carton or yogurt cups

Pipe cleaners

Sequins, buttons, or beads

White craft glue

Safety scissors

HERE'S WHAT YOU DO

1 Spread your materials in front of you. Do you see the makings for a Crazy Critter?

2 Remember Crazy Critters come right from your imagination. Use sections of the egg carton to make a caterpillar-type body or a roly-poly body.

3 Attach pipe cleaners for arms, legs, antennae—or for crazy hair! Use sequins, buttons, or beads for eyes. Use the glue to assemble your sculpture.

LET IT POUR!

✳ Read about imaginary creatures in Dr. Seuss's books. Pick a name for your critter and make up a story about it.

✳ Ask a grown-up to make a batch of salt dough or baking soda clay. Sculpt a wacky animal or pet.

✳ Visit a museum or look at books to search out sculpture. Look for Rodin's masterpieces and ballerina sculptures by Degas.

LIGHTNING BOLT!

✳ There are some very unusual, real animals whose appearances might surprise you. Go to a zoo, if you can, or look in some animal books or *National Geographic* magazines at the library. Do you see anything unusual like an **armadillo** in its suit of armor or a **rhinoceros** wallowing in the mud? Even the graceful **giraffe** is quite a surprising creature.

Snip Art

Here's some art fun in the Japanese style of paper folding and cutting.

HERE'S WHAT YOU NEED

Origami paper or squares of wrapping paper

Pencil

Safety scissors

HERE'S WHAT YOU DO

1 Fold a paper square in half. Draw a half circle about 3 inches (7.5 cm) on the folded edges. Around the circle draw a scalloped border.

2 Cut out the outside scalloped edge and then the inside part of the half-circle, creating a fancy bracelet when opened.

make a snowflake!

folded edge

fold

fold

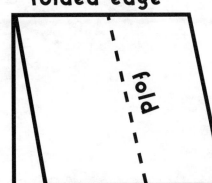

fold

fold

folded edge

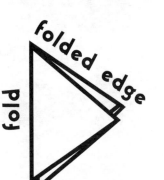

LET IT POUR!

❋ Listen to *The Crane Wife* retold by Sumiko Yagawa and *Tree of Cranes* by Allan Say.

❋ Ask a grown-up to help you make a snowflake out of paper. Hang it from string in your window.

LIGHTNING BOLT!

✳ Paper cutting is popular in many countries. *Kirigami* is the Japanese art of paper cutting (*kiri* means cutting and *gami* means paper in Japanese). In some European countries, very detailed designs of flowers, hearts, and birds are cut to decorate boxes and furniture. Some children in other countries are taught paper-cutting techniques in school.

GIGGLES and WIGGLES

Giggles seem to start with a grin and grow until laughter just comes spilling out. Here you'll find giggles, grins, silliness, and plenty of fun of every kind.

Rainy Day Backwards Party

We've all walked backward, or worn our baseball caps backward, but have you ever done everything backward? You're sure to have a giggling good time!

HERE'S WHAT YOU NEED

A few friends

Paper and crayons

Large mirror nearby

Refreshments including sand-
wiches and dessert

HERE'S WHAT YOU DO

1 Invite some friends over and ask them to wear their clothes back-ward. Greet them at the door say-ing, "Good-bye."

2 Everyone print or trace their names on a piece of paper with crayons. Ask a grown-up to help. Then hold the piece of paper in front of a mir-ror. What do you notice?

3 Next, serve a backward meal—you guessed it, eating the dessert first! Eat with your opposite hand.

4 Tell riddles and knock, knock jokes—backward! Give the answer first and ask your friends to make up the question or joke. When the party's over, say "Hello!"

LET IT POUR!

✳ Make up a secret backward language. Here's one way: Take a sentence like "run to the store." Add the sound "ay" to the end of every word. "Run to the store" becomes "Runay toay theay storeay." Now you try it.

✳ Ask a grown-up to read you a favorite story beginning at the back of the book. Can you guess what is going to happen next?

LIGHTNING BOLT!

✳ When you learn to read English, you will begin at the front of the book and read each line moving your eyes from left to right. In the Hebrew language, however, you would begin at the back of the book and read each line from right to left. So backward in English is frontward in Hebrew!

Silly Tongue Twisters

Does your tongue ever get twisted up so that funny words spill out of your mouth? Well, here are some tongue twisters that will give you the giggles.

HERE'S WHAT YOU NEED

Index cards

Markers

HERE'S WHAT YOU DO

1 Think of a silly tongue twister or make one up. Here are three to get you started:

She sells seashells at the seashore.

Peter Piper picked a peck of pickled peppers.

Rubber baby buggy bumpers.

2 Draw a picture that will remind you of it, like a picture of sea-shells.

3 Ask a grown-up to write down the tongue twister on the back of the card.

4 Then hold up the card. Can you remember the tongue twist-er from the picture? If not, a grown-up can read it for you. Everyone practice saying it together slowly.

5 After you have practiced a bit, go full speed ahead. How many times can you say your tongue twister without making an error? If you can say it more times than anyone else without making a mistake, you win that card. Then go on to the next card.

The chatty chicken and the chummy chimp rode on the choo choo.

LET IT POUR!

✳ Make up your own tongue twist-ers. Think of words that start with the same letter. How fast can you say them?

✳ Make a tongue-twister collage. Cut out pictures of words that all begin with the same sound like **ch**icken, **ch**atty, **ch**imp, **ch**oo **ch**oo. Then make up a silly tongue twister using everything in your collage. "The chatty chicken and the chummy chimp rode on the choo choo."

Be a Clown

Here's your chance to really clown around!

HERE'S WHAT YOU NEED

Paper plate

Markers

Hole punch

Yarn

Some oversized clothes

(ask a grown-up)

HERE'S WHAT YOU DO

1 Draw a clown face on the bottom of your paper plate with your markers. Ask a grown-up to poke a hole on each side of the plate for the yarn ties and eyeholes, too. Tie the yarn on.

2 Dress up in some big clothes. Tie your clown mask around your head.

3 Think about what a clown does to make people laugh. Try a dance or a song, do a somersault, plant a big kiss on someone's cheek, or just act goofy!

LET IT POUR!

✷ Look at the wonderful circus pictures in *Circus* by Peter Spier.

✷ Make your own paper plate tambourine. Jingle and jangle, stamp and shake, you'll be surprised at the music you make!

✷ Cut out huge clown feet from construction paper and ask a grown-up to help tie them to your feet.

Knock, Knock

Knock, knock. Who's there? Just me with a great knock, knock joke especially for you!

HERE'S WHAT YOU NEED

Pencil

Paper

Crayons

Hole punch

Yarn

HERE'S WHAT YOU DO

1 Knock, knock jokes have a set pattern:

You: "Knock, knock."

They: "Who's there?"

You think of something funny to say like: "Banana."

They: "Banana, who?"

You: "Banana split!"

2 Sit down with some friends and make up funny knock, knock jokes. Then draw a picture on the top of the page that reminds you of the joke. Ask a grown-up to write the joke on the bottom half of the page.

3 Punch holes in the side of the papers and tie with yarn for a great Knock, Knock Joke Book.

LET IT POUR!

❊ Instead of knock, knock jokes, collect riddles in a Riddle Book. Ask everyone at dinner to think of at least one funny riddle to add to your book.

❊ For a lot of giggles, read *Riddle-icious* by J. Patrick Lewis and *Why Did the Chicken Cross the Road and Other Riddles Old & New* by Joanna Cole.

Silly Story Circle

Share a silly story with your friends and see who has the last word.

HERE'S WHAT YOU DO

1 Pick an animal or a person—like a bunny or a police officer—to be the main character in your story.

2 Because the story is going to be silly, quietly think of the silly things this character can do. Use your imagination.

3 One person begins the story by saying something about the character; then the next person adds something to the story. Continue taking turns creating a story about the character. How silly can you make your story?

LET IT POUR!

✽ All the storytellers make up a title for the story and decide what would be on the cover of the storybook. Then each of you draw your own storybook cover.

✽ No one to play Silly Story with? Start a silly story with a grown-up at home. See how long you can keep your story going. Continue adding a few sentences every day.

LIGHTNING BOLT!

✽ Many books that you listen to contain stories that are **make-believe**. The story didn't really happen; it is **pretend**. Some books are about **true** things like a book about how a baby chick hatches. Sometimes it is hard to tell pretend stories and true stories apart. Ask a librarian to help you pick out one make-believe story and one true story.

silly story

Shake the Sillies Out

Stomp like an elephant, sway like a tree, or just kick up your heels and dance to the beat!

HERE'S WHAT YOU NEED

A variety of music

Open space

HERE'S WHAT YOU DO

1. Listen to some music. Does the music make you think of something? How does it make you feel?

2. Move your body to the beat of the music. Does the music make you want to sway like an elephant's trunk, leap like a graceful deer, or fly like an airplane?

3. Go with the music, sway to the slow parts and gallop to the fast parts, changing as the music changes.

LET IT POUR!

✳ Pretend you are the wind. Move your body as if you are a warm summer breeze, then try to move like you are a howling windstorm. Try moving like other things: be water rushing down a stream, a gentle wave rolling on a sandy beach, or a light snowfall that turns into a blizzard!

✳ Watch the video "Dance Along with George Balanchine's *The Nutcracker*" (1993, Warner Home Video) and then—dance along!

Perfectly Preposterous Parade

Put on some marching music and strut your stuff!

HERE'S WHAT YOU NEED

A variety of music

Open space

HERE'S WHAT YOU DO

1 Put on some marching music and become the bandleader, the drummer, or the flag bearer in your own parade.

2 March from room to room. Stand tall and march to the beat.

LET IT POUR!

❋ Make your own marching instruments. Try a pie tin drum, a rolled newspaper baton, or a bag-and-beans rhythm shaker to add to the music.

❋ Sing "The Ants Go Marching" as you parade through your house.

KITCHEN CONNECTION

The kitchen is a great place to explore, create, and have fun. Here are some good-time activities for you to enjoy and some yummy treats to eat, too.

Scratch and Sniff Painting

Here's a way to make your painting look good—and smell good, too!

HERE'S WHAT YOU NEED

Fruit-flavored gelatin

Paper

Newspaper

Paintbrush

Watercolor paints

Craft glue

HERE'S WHAT YOU DO

1 Place your paper on a sheet of newspaper. Use the watercolors to paint a fruity picture. Look at a bowl of apples and bananas to help you. Let your painting dry.

2 After your fruit picture is dry, spread the craft glue over each of your fruits. Sprinkle powdered, fruit-flavored gelatin over the wet craft glue.

3 Let your picture dry. The craft glue will dry clear and you will be left with a sweet-smelling picture.

LET IT POUR!

✳ How many different kinds of fruit can you name? Which ones are your favorites?

✳ Make a fruit salad with a grown-up. You can peel the bananas and wash the grapes, while someone else cuts the fruits. Toss and eat!

✳ Play a guessing game with fruit. Someone names a fruit like strawberries, and everyone else names their favorite way to eat it like "on cereal" or "in ice cream" or "freshly picked from the fields."

LIGHTNING BOLT!

✳ Depending on what part of North America you live in, you might have different fruit growing outside. Can you pick lemons from your trees? The answer is yes if you live in California. Is apple season a special time of year? It is if you live in Vermont, New York, or Washington. If you can pick a juicy orange right in your backyard, you may very well live in Florida.

71

Bread People

Here's a way to make your very own play people—out of bread! When they're finished they'll be great to play with, but too hard to eat.

HERE'S WHAT YOU NEED

1 cup (250 ml) water

1 cup (250 ml) salt

3 cups (750 ml) flour

Mixing bowl

Toothpicks

Garlic press

72

HERE'S WHAT YOU DO

1 Mix all the ingredients together in the mixing bowl.

2 Knead the dough until it's smooth. The dough should feel rubbery and smooth when it is ready to form into Bread People. Do you like the way it feels on your hands?

3 Make a ball from the dough for the body. Make a smaller ball for the head. Connect the two using a drop of water.

4 Roll the dough to make arms and legs. Press a small amount of dough through the garlic press to form hair. Attach the arms, legs, and hair to the body using a little water.

5 Add clothes using more dough and draw a face with a toothpick.

6 Ask a grown-up to bake your bread people in an oven for 2—3 hours at 275°F (140°C).

7 Let cool and paint with tempera paint, if you wish.

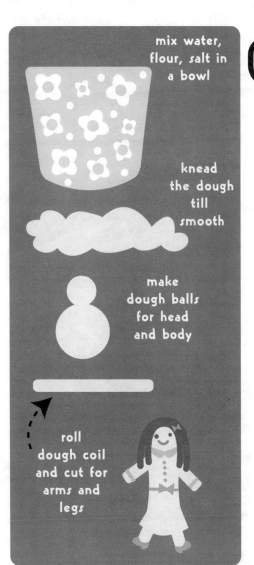

mix water, flour, salt in a bowl

knead the dough till smooth

make dough balls for head and body

roll dough coil and cut for arms and legs

LET IT POUR!

❋ To make refrigerator magnets, cut out the dough with cookie cutters. (If the dough sticks to the cookie cutters, spray them with a nonstick cooking spray.) After they are baked, paint them, add glitter, and glue a magnet to the back.

❋ Make all kinds of Bread People and Bread Animals, wearing costumes and uniforms. How could you make the fur on a kitty?

❋ Listen to the story about the gingerbread boy and then make some gingerbread cookies for a yummy rainy day snack.

Winnie-the-Pooh Picnic

You don't need a sunny day for a picnic. Just spread a blanket inside and enjoy everything—except the ants!

HERE'S WHAT YOU NEED

Blanket

Peanut butter

Honey

Muffins

Winnie-the-Pooh books

HERE'S WHAT YOU DO

1 Spread your blanket on the floor. Ask a grown-up to help you spread the peanut butter and honey on your muffins. Bring along your favorite drinks.

2 Invite your stuffed animals to join your picnic. Read from your Winnie-the-Pooh books and watch the rain fall on the windowpanes. Pretend you are one of Pooh's friends on this rainy day. How would each one behave at the picnic?

LET IT POUR!

❋ Read the chapter of A. A. Milne's *Winnie-the-Pooh* titled "In Which Piglet Is Entirely Surrounded by Water."

❋ Make up your own melody and sing Pooh's song, "I'm Just a Little Black Rain Cloud."

❋ Christopher Robin used to watch the raindrops race down the window. Pick your own racing raindrops and watch to see which one wins the race to the windowsill.

LIGHTNING BOLT!

❋ A. A. Milne wrote the Winnie-the-Pooh stories in 1926. Children of all ages have been listening to them ever since. Talk to some friends and talk to some older people, too, about their favorite adventures of Pooh and their favorite Pooh characters. Two wonderful collections of poems by A. A. Milne are *Now We Are Six* and *When We Were Very Young*. See if you can find them in the library.

Butter in a Jar

You can make your very own butter—just as folks did long ago—and share it with your family for dinner or with classmates for a snack.

HERE'S WHAT YOU NEED

1/2 cup (125 ml) heavy cream

1 tablespoon (15 ml) sour cream

Lidded jar

Spoon

Saucer

Salt (optional)

HERE'S WHAT YOU DO

1 Pour the cream and sour cream into the jar.

2 Cover the jar tightly and shake it hard. Keep shaking or take turns shaking with a few people. Watch the liquids as you shake them up. After a long while, you will see a lump of soft butter at the bottom of the jar.

3 Carefully pour off the leftover liquid and place the butter in a saucer. Press the butter firmly with the rounded back of a spoon, draining the water. (If you like salted butter, sprinkle some on the butter.) Guess what? You have made your own delicious butter!

pour cream and spoon sour cream into jar

screw on lid and shake shake shake

when lump forms pour out liquid

place butter on a saucer and press with a spoon

LET IT POUR!

❋ Have a tea party serving tea, toast, your homemade butter, and jam!

❋ Listen to *Lucy's Christmas* and *Lucy's Summer* by Donald Hall to hear about other activities and games children played long ago.

Perfectly Easy Pretzels

Salty, doughy pretzels are a favorite treat for many people. Here's a pretzel with a little different twist!

HERE'S WHAT YOU NEED

Refrigerated biscuit dough

Cinnamon

Brown sugar

Cookie sheet

Rolling pin

HERE'S WHAT YOU DO

1 Using a rolling pin, roll out the refrigerated dough.

2 Ask a grown-up to cut the dough into long, fat strips.

3 Place two strips side by side and twist them together. Then, shape your pretzel into the traditional pretzel shape, your initials, or any other shape.

4 Sprinkle on the brown sugar and cinnamon, place on a cookie sheet, and bake following the package directions.

LET IT POUR!

* When you buy a bag of pretzels in the grocery store they are usually right next to the potato chips. What is the **same** about chips and pretzels and what is **different**?

* Your brown sugar and cinnamon pretzels have a **sweet** taste. What taste do most pretzels have?

* If you had a choice among pretzels, potato chips, or popcorn for a snack, which one would you choose?

LIGHTNING BOLT!

* Pretzels were first made in Germany many years ago by monks. They were given to children as a reward for learning their prayers. The pretzel twist that we all are familiar with was created to look like the crossed arms of a child praying.

Unbirthday Party

Why wait until your birthday to have a party?

HERE'S WHAT YOU NEED

Construction paper

Yarn

Crayons

HERE'S WHAT YOU DO

1 Before your party ask a grown-up to help you bake cupcakes. Leave them unfrosted.

2 Decide what yout party will celebrate. You might choose to celebrate nature.

3 Make party hats by out of a large piece of construction paper. Ask a grown-up to staple or tape the hat together. Add a yarn strap and hat decorations that go with your theme.

4 Draw a big picture of your theme for a game of Pin-the-Tail-On. At a nature party, you might draw a picture of a big tree and then pin leaves on it.

5 With a grown-up's help, frost the cupcakes and decorate them with sprinkles, chocolate chips, and raisins. Now, eat them!

ALL ABOUT ME

You may think you know everything there is to know about yourself. After all, you spend more time with you than anyone else! Everyone is changing all the time—changing their minds, changing what they like and dislike, or changing how they appear. Here are some fun things to do to find out all about you—as you are today!

Giant Paper Person

How would you like a giant paper person that looks just like you to hang in your room or on your door?

HERE'S WHAT YOU NEED

A partner

A roll of paper, 36 inches (90cm) wide

Crayons

Scissors

HERE'S WHAT YOU DO

1   Ask someone to help you roll out the paper to a length longer than your height.

2   Lie down on the paper. Ask your partner to trace around your body on the paper with a crayon.

3   Cut out your body shape with the scissors. Color your life-size person wearing your favorite clothes! If you want, you can add yarn for hair and other decorations.

LET IT POUR!

✳ Double the paper before you cut it. Then staple both cutouts together, leaving a small opening to stuff with crumpled newspaper for a three-dimensional paper person.

✳ Make a shadow drawing by taping a large sheet of white paper on a wall. Place a light in front of the object or person you want to draw. Trace the shadow with a crayon.

✳ Make photo puppets of your family or friends: Ask a grown-up to help you cut out the faces of family members from some extra photos. Glue the faces to the tops of Popsicle sticks. Make clothes for your puppet out of construction paper and glue them to the stick. Arms can be made from pipe cleaners. Put on a puppet show about your family or friends.

LIGHTNING BOLT!

✳ People come in all different shapes and sizes. Sometimes people wish they could be shaped like someone else, but the truth is there are good things about being just the way you are. The most important reason is that you are the only person in the whole world who looks exactly like you. People love you for being you!

My Friendship Tree

Here's some fun, just wait and see, when you create a friendship tree!

HERE'S WHAT YOU NEED

Large piece of poster board

Markers

Construction paper

Scissors

Craft glue

HERE'S WHAT YOU DO

1 Ask a grown-up to help you draw a large tree with lots of branches—but no leaves—on your poster board.

2 Draw leaf shapes on the construction paper and cut them out.

3 Make leaves for all your friends by drawing a picture of something they like to do and then, with a grown-up's help, writing their names, one on each leaf.

4 Who should you include? Maybe the people in your class, or the people who live on your street, or the people who live in your house.

LET IT POUR!

✳ Make a tree for your family or the people you live with. Along with parents, grandparents, sisters and brothers, don't forget to include your pets!

✳ Play a Friendship Tree game. Ask everyone to think of something funny that happened to them. Share your stories. Which was the silliest?

✳ Ask your older friends or family members to tell you about their favorite toys and games when they were your age.

LIGHTNING BOLT!

✳ Sometimes we feel that we have a whole lot of friends and sometimes we feel that we don't have any friends. There are lots of ways to become someone's friend. You can play with them, share with them, help them with a chore, wait for them when they are busy, listen to them, and laugh with them. And friends don't have to be people—your pets and favorite books can be your friends, too.

Exploring Me

Here's a new way to look at yourself—without mirrors.

HERE'S WHAT YOU NEED

A grown-up partner

HERE'S WHAT YOU DO

1 Pretend there are no mirrors. Ask a grown-up to sit in front of you and let your hands tell you about your face.

2 Place one hand on your face and one hand on the grown-up's face. Gently touch the grown-up's chin, then touch your own. Do they feel **alike**? How are they **different**?

3 Touch the grown-up's nose, then touch your nose. Are they the same or different? Continue exploring your face by comparing ears, eyebrows, and lips.

LET IT POUR!

✳ Without looking in a mirror, draw a picture of yourself. Look in a mirror and compare what you see with what you remembered. Are you happy in your picture? What are the clues that you are happy or sad?

✳ Look at the pictures in *A Child's Book of Art* selected by Lucy Micklethwait. Are there any pictures of people? What did the artist tell you about people in the picture?

✳ If there were no mirrors, what are some other ways that you might still be able to see your reflection?

My Favorites

Here's a chance to think about your favorites—people, things, thoughts, experiences—and put them all together in a book that you can save forever and ever.

HERE'S WHAT YOU NEED

Paper

Crayons

Stapler or yarn

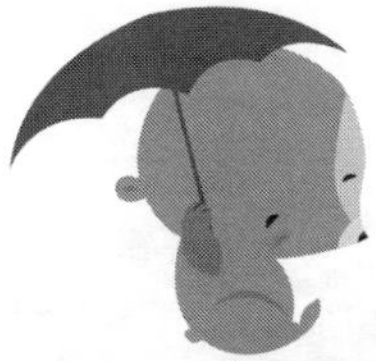

HERE'S WHAT YOU DO

1 Everyone has different ideas about what is special, or favorite, to them. It could be the sound of your kitty purring on your bed, a special card that is fuzzy on the outside, or a toy you have had a long time.

2 Think about your favorites. Do you have a favorite pet, toy, food, color, or season? How about a favorite friend or grown-up? Talk about what makes each favorite thing or person so special to you.

3 Draw pictures of your favorites on separate pieces of paper.

4 Ask a grown-up to staple your pages together or tie them together with yarn so you will have a book of favorites. What would you like to put on the cover of your book?

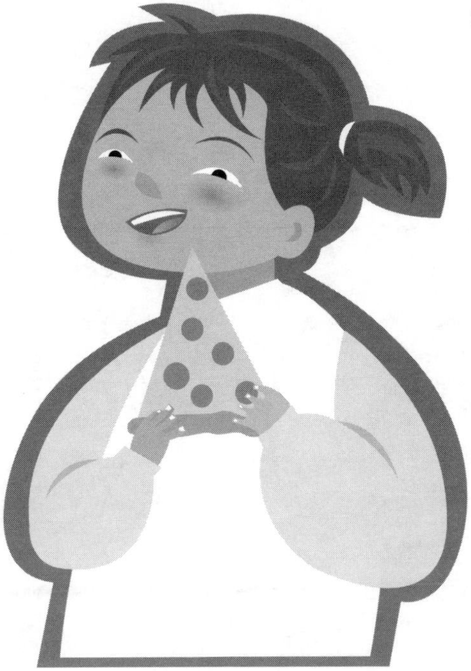

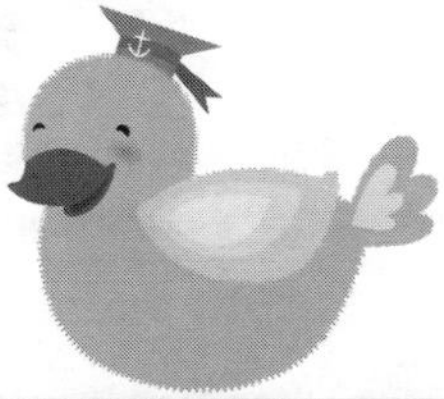

LET IT POUR!

- Can you guess someone else's favorites—like their favorite foods, or stories, or baseball cap? What are the clues that help you make a good guess?
- What are your least favorite things? What food or color don't you like? Why don't you like them?
- Try something new a few times. How does it rate on your "favorite meter"? It just might become a favorite after all.

Hands and Feet

We use our hands and feet for so many things. Take a closer look at both.

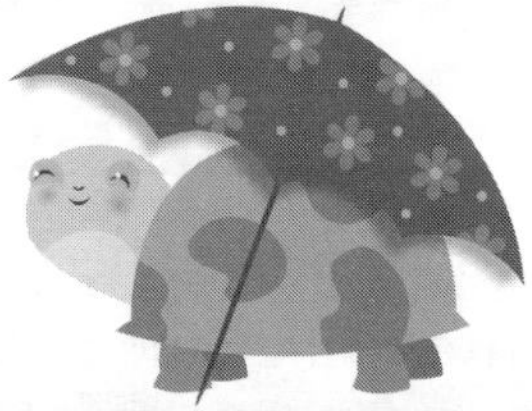

HERE'S WHAT YOU NEED

Paper

Crayons

Ruler (measuring stick)

LET IT POUR!

* Count all the fingers on one hand and then all the toes on one foot. How many fingers do you have in all? How many toes?

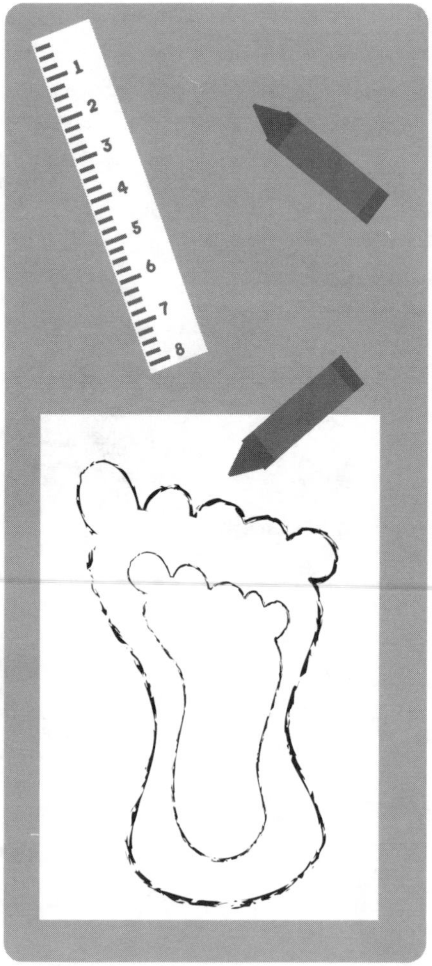

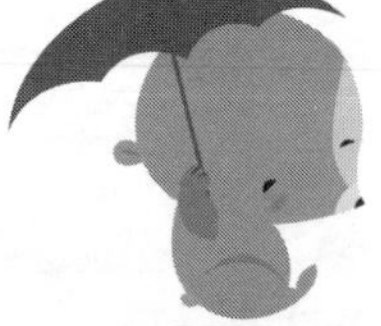

HERE'S WHAT YOU DO

1 Trace your bare foot on the paper with a crayon. Trace a grown-up's foot also.

2 Ask a grown-up to help you measure the two footprints with your ruler. Which one is bigger? Do you think you could fit your footprint inside of theirs?

3 Next, trace your hands. What is the same and what is different about your hands and feet?

4 Ask a grown-up if you can try on his or her shoes. What do you notice about wearing big shoes? Now, try on a pair of grown-up gloves or mittens.

COLORS and SHAPES

When you look around, there are so many wonderful colors and unusual shapes everywhere. There are tangerine orange and midnight blue, plus circles, diamonds, and hearts just for you!

Mixing It Up!

Rainy days are often gray days because the sun isn't shining brightly. There are lots of ways to brighten a gray day including creating your own colors.

HERE'S WHAT YOU NEED

Popsicle sticks

Finger paints

Paper

HERE'S WHAT YOU DO

1   Using a Popsicle stick, scoop out some yellow finger paint in a small circle onto the paper. Then, with a clean Popsicle stick, scoop out some blue finger paint onto the other side of the paper.

2   Now take a little yellow and a little blue and mix them together in a new circle. What color did you make?

3   Take a fresh piece of paper, and do the same thing, only this time begin with a circle of yellow again and a circle of red. What new color did you make?

4   What other colors can you make?

LET IT POUR!

✳ Ask a grown-up to cut up a sponge into different shapes. Use the sponge shapes to stamp on your paper with your new paint colors.

✳ Explore the different colors around your house or classroom. Open up a closet and see how many different colors you can count.

LIGHTNING BOLT!

✳ If you look around you—right this very minute—how many colors do you see? Five? Ten? There are actually hundreds of different colors—just look in a Crayola crayon box! You may be very surprised to learn that all these colors actually begin with the three basic colors that you used in Mixing It Up!—red, yellow, and blue.

Rainbow Mobile

A rainbow after a summer shower is always a wonderful sight. Here's a way to have a rainbow to brighten every day.

HERE'S WHAT YOU NEED

Construction paper (rainbow colors)

Markers

Safety scissors

Ruler

Clothes hanger

Yarn or string

Crayons

HERE'S WHAT YOU DO

1 Draw a big circle, square, triangle, and a diamond on different-colored pieces of construction paper.

2 Ask a grown-up to help you cut them out and poke a hole in the top of each one. Create your mobile by pulling the yarn through the hole and tying the shapes onto the hanger so they dangle.

3 Draw a huge rainbow arc on a large piece of white paper. Color it with bands of colors. Ask a grown-up to cut it out and hang it from your mobile.

LET IT POUR!

✳ Cut out a squiggle from construction paper, by cutting a circular snake pattern (beginning on the outside moving inward). Add it to your mobile.

✳ Here's a way to make a double-decker rainbow mobile. Cut out a large rainbow and shapes. Hang your shapes from the ends of the rainbow arc.

LIGHTNING BOLT!

✳ Every rainbow seems to look different depending on where you are standing, how hard it rained, and how brightly the sun is shining through. But actually, all rainbows have the exact same colors in them and the colors are always seen in the same order. Isn't that a surprise?

Picture Perfect Shapes

Frame your favorite photo with the shape of your choice for these fun-to-make frames.

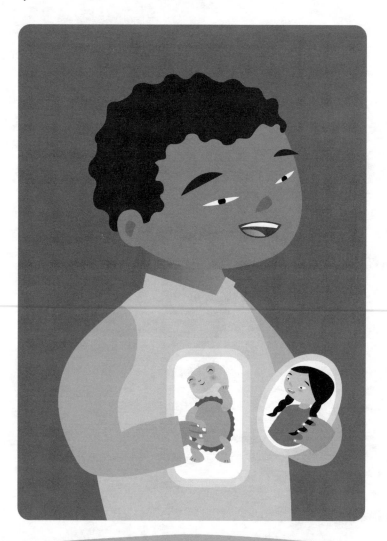

Poster board

Marker

Photos

Safety scissors

Craft glue

1 Draw some shapes on the poster board. Place the photo on the shape to make sure the shape will fit around the picture.

2 Cut out the shapes with a grown-up's help. Then place your photo in the middle of the shape so that there is a border all around.

3 Use your finger to apply glue to the border of your picture. Place the photo on the shape again, only this time press down and then let dry.

4 When dry, hang on a bulletin board or on your bedroom door.

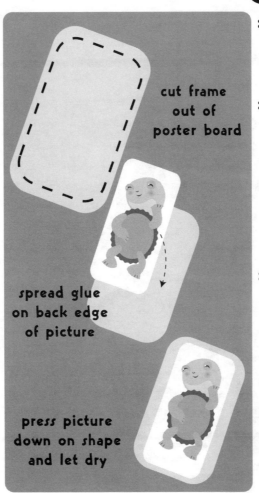

cut frame out of poster board

spread glue on back edge of picture

press picture down on shape and let dry

LET IT POUR!

✻ Attach a magnet, pin, or a folded piece of cardboard to the back for a stand to complete your frame.

✻ Do a photo sort. Ask if you can have some of the doubles of photos at home. Then make a sorting plan. You can sort by subject (all pictures of you in one pile, all of your dog in another), by event, by year, or by time of year.

✻ Begin a personal photo album. Sort your photos (see above) and then carefully glue them onto construction paper. Bind with a yarn tie.

Shape Mosaic

A mosaic is a picture made with little pieces. The pieces can be of any-thing—bits of tile, tissue paper, tiny pebbles, different colored macaroni. Here you will be using construction paper to make a Shape Mosaic.

1 With a grown-up's help, cut out a large triangle from construction paper. Next, using assorted colors of paper, cut out some medium-sized triangles. Then, cut out a bunch of small triangles in differ-ent colors.

2 Glue the medium triangles all over the large triangle. Fit as many on as you can. Then, glue lots of small triangles inside the medium tri-angles, placing the small triangles very close together.

3 Now you have a mosaic using three different sizes of triangles.

HERE'S WHAT YOU NEED

**Construction paper
(assorted colors)
Safety scissors
Craft glue**

LET IT POUR!

* Make another Shape Mosaic using large and medium-sized circles, only this time fill the medium-sized circles with buttons glued on for a new kind of mosaic.

* You can make a very pretty mosaic by drawing a huge shape or large flower. Then paste on small pieces of torn tissue paper.

LIGHTNING BOLT!

* When someone asks us to name two or three shapes, most of us will say **circle, square**, and **triangle**. Sometimes we forget that there are many shapes besides those three. Think of the eight-sided shape of a STOP sign, or the four-sided rectangle of a cereal box. Can you think of any other shapes?

Terrific Tie-Dye

All it takes are a few squirts of color, a few twists and ties, and you can make a new shirt that is full of color.

HERE'S WHAT YOU NEED

Rubber bands or string

White T-shirt or socks

Cold-water dye, non-toxic

Old basin or bucket

Old dish detergent bottles

HERE'S WHAT YOU DO

1 Hold your T-shirt or socks with both hands and begin folding and twisting the fabric. Ask a grown-up to help you tie the fabric with string or wrap rubber bands tightly around the fabric.

2 Mix the cold-water dye in the bucket. Fill the empty detergent bottles with the dye. Squirt the colors onto the fabric. (If it's not raining too hard, try this step outside!) Ask a grown-up to follow the directions on the dye to set the colors into the fabric so they won't wash away.

3 Unwrap the tie-dyed shirt or socks and hang up to dry.

1, 2, 3 COUNT WITH ME!

You may not know it but you are already counting. Do you sometimes ask for two pieces of candy or three more pushes on the swing? That's what counting is all about—putting numbers to work!

Guess How Many?

When you make a good guess, you think about the question and try to figure out the answer before guessing. Sometimes, though, it is fun to make out-of-this-world guesses!

HERE'S WHAT YOU NEED

Paper

Crayons

HERE'S WHAT YOU DO

1. Here is a guessing game that you can play at home, in school, or even in the car. Decide what things you are going to try to Guess How Many? If you are at home, you might guess how many steps go upstairs, how many doors are inside the house, or how many pots are in the cupboard.

2. Draw a picture with some crayons of each thing you are going to guess. Then, make some guesses and put marks for the number you guess next to each picture (six pots would have six lines next to the pot picture).

3. Now, count how many of each thing are really there and mark that number with a different-colored crayon. How close were your guesses?

LET IT POUR!

* Draw a picture of your house from memory. Then walk through your house and compare your picture with what you see.

* Count other things in your house like doorknobs, chairs, pictures, and windows. Do you have more windows or doors? Do you have fewer chairs or beds?

* Find out how many eggs are in a dozen.

* Make a Days-of-the-Week bracelet. Take a piece of yarn and on Sunday string on one bead or piece of macaroni. Add one every day until you get to Sunday again. How many beads are on your bracelet?

LIGHTNING BOLT!

* When people make a **wild guess**, it means they have no idea what the answer is. When people make a **thoughtful guess**, they use clues to get closer to the exact answer. If someone asked you how many glasses of milk you drink a day, you might use the clue "I drink milk at every meal" and then make a thoughtful guess of three.

Tick Tock, Make a Clock

There are so many things to like about clocks! Play ones are fun to make, broken ones are fun to take apart, cuckoo clocks are fun to watch, and grandfather clocks are fun to listen to. Best of all, they keep track of the time for us.

HERE'S WHAT YOU NEED

Paper plate

Markers

Safety scissors

Cardboard or construction paper

Paper fasteners

HERE'S WHAT YOU DO

1 Look at a clock. Do you see the numbers 1 through 12?

2 Now, trace over a grown-up's numbers or draw your own numbers on a plate just as they appear on the clock. This is the **face** of the clock.

3 Cut two strips of cardboard for the **hands** of your clock. Make one a little shorter than the other and cut them with pointed ends.

4 Use the paper fastener to attach the hands to the center of the clock face. Now you can move them to show the time.

LET IT POUR!

- Learning to tell time takes a lot of practice. To help you get started, ask a grown-up to set the hands on your homemade clock to a special time, like 6:00 for dinnertime. Now, when you see a real clock with its hands in the same position, you will know it is time for dinner.
- Is there a broken clock or an old watch around your house or classroom? Maybe you can look inside to see all the gears that make the clock go.
- Do you think a clock sound is "tick tock"? What does a clock sound say to you?

LIGHTNING BOLT!

- Clocks tell us the time of the day or night. They tell us when to get up in the morning, when to go to school, and when it is bedtime. There are all sorts of different clocks such as **alarm clocks, wristwatches, stopwatches, pocket watches, cuckoo clocks, grandfather clocks,** and **clock radios**. Visiting a clock shop can be very noisy if they are "tick-tocking" at once.

Measuring Madness

Measure by measure, this is sure to bring you oodles, gallons, and yards of fun.

HERE'S WHAT YOU NEED

**Measuring tools: ruler,
measuring cup, scale**

Cereal

Water

HERE'S WHAT YOU DO

1 Look at the different measuring tools. What do you think they would each be best at measuring?

2 Try measuring the cereal with each tool. Which tools work best at measuring cereal?

3 Measure ɪ cup (250 ml) of water in the measuring cup. Could you measure the water with a ruler? What does a cup of water weigh?

LET IT POUR!

* No measuring tools? Use your hand or foot to measure. How many hands high is a chair? How many feet wide is the hallway?

* Talk about other measurement tools. What does a clock measure? A thermometer? A calendar? The sun?

* Make up a size measurement and call it a gleeb. How many gleebs long is a pencil? Your foot?

LIGHTNING BOLT!

* Ask a grown-up to help you start an "I'm Growing Wall." On the first day of each month, stand straight and tall against the wall. Ask someone to mark a line where your head touches the wall. Then put the date next to it. Some months you will stay the same and some months you will grow. How much did you grow in a year?

Number Detective

There are so many numbers hiding throughout your house and classroom.
How many can you find?

HERE'S WHAT YOU NEED

Paper

Pencil

Markers

HERE'S WHAT YOU DO

1 Search your house or classroom for numbers! Look at clocks, envelopes, computers, radios, phones, measuring cups—even pencils!

2 Ask a grown-up to write the numbers 1 through 12 nice and large on a piece of paper. You trace over them in markers.

3 Now, be a Number Detective. Every time you see one of those numbers put a check mark next to it.

4 Count up your check marks. Which number did you find most often? Which numbers didn't you find anywhere?

LET IT POUR!

✳ Practice tracing or writing the numbers 1, 2, 3.

✳ Celebrate a number each week. If it is "3" week, do everything in threes. Decorate your house with threes. Read three poems at bedtime. Eat your three favorite foods. Put all your pennies in piles of three. Have three crackers for a snack.

✳ Listen to *One, Two, Three, Count with Me* by Catherine and Laurence Anholt.

One, Two, Three

Here's a counting game that's as easy as counting 1, 2, 3!

HERE'S WHAT YOU NEED

A partner

12 3
Go!

HERE'S WHAT YOU DO

1 Two players sit face-to-face and count 1, 2, 3, go!

2 On the word *go*, both players lower their arms and show one, two, or three fingers. Just as you lower yours, call out same or different.

3 If both players display the same finger number, then the player that called same is the winner. If the finger numbers are different, then the caller of different wins. If both call the same thing, then no one wins.

LET IT POUR!

* Learn how to count in another language. In Japanese, 1, 2, 3 is *eechee, nee, sahn*. In Italian, 1, 2, 3 is *uno, due, tre*. In Spanish, 1, 2, 3 is *uno, dos, tres*.

* Play Higher-Lower. Call out a number and say higher (or lower). The other person has to answer with an appropriate number.

uno, due, tre!

eechee, nee, sahn!

LIGHTNING BOLT!

* Jan-Kem-Po is a Japanese counting game that is played in pairs. (You may know it by Paper-Scissors-Stone or Rock-Paper-Scissors). To play, practice these hand movements first: a closed fist represents stone, a fist with two fingers extended is scissors, an open hand is paper. The two players, hand in the stone position with arm bent at the elbows, say Jan-Kem-Po; on Po the players show stone, scissors, or paper. The player wins as follows: stone breaks scissors, scissors cuts paper, and paper wraps around stone. The ultimate winner wins two out of three rounds.

113

Flip!

Most everyone enjoys playing cards. Here's a card game that is good number fun, too.

Playing cards

Partner(s)

✻ Play the same game with the lowest card winning the hand.

✻ Play Before and After Dominoes. For example, if a three is showing, instead of matching a three, the player can put down a two or a four.

1 Remove all the picture cards from the deck and set aside. Deal the same number of cards to everyone from the remaining cards.

2 Someone calls out "flip" and everyone turns over a card. The player who has the highest card wins the round and collects all the turned-over cards. If there is a tie, split the cards evenly.

3 When all the cards are gone, the player with the most cards wins.

FUN and GAMES

Everyone's idea of fun is different. You may enjoy running in the wind or splashing in a puddle. Or, at another time, a good game of tag or musical chairs may be just the thing!

All-of-a-Kind

This old favorite is a great way to have fun on a rainy day! You can play with one partner or a lot of partners–or challenge yourself to a game.

all of a kind

tap - tap

rabbit

116

HERE'S WHAT YOU DO

1 Sit in a circle of friends or with a partner. Set a slow beat by patting the floor with your hands.

2 Start off the game by saying "All-of-a-Kind" to the two sets of two beats, "such as" to the next two. Then, someone picks a category, or kind, of thing, such as colors, shapes, animals, or letters.

All-of-: (2 beats)

a-kind: (2 beats)

such-as: (2 beats)

col-ors: (2 beats)

gre-en (2 beats)

re-ed (2 beats)

pur-ple (2 beats)

3 As you go around the circle, each player must say something from that category in the next two beats. When someone gets stumped, change categories and begin again.

guinea pig

pat - pat

LET IT POUR!

❋ Pair up and play the same game, but instead of naming all-of-a-kind, say opposites. If the first player says "up," the second player would say "down."

❋ Play with a partner but instead of taking turns, one partner says all the things in one category and the other counts how many are named. Then, switch roles with a new category.

Downpour

Here's a perfect way to spend a rainy day with your friends!

pat pat

tap tap

**3 or more people
(4 works best!)**

HERE'S WHAT YOU DO

1 Sit in a circle on the floor. Choose a sound—like rain falling. The first person begins as if the rain is starting to fall (by rubbing thumbs and fingers together), the next will be slightly louder (rubbing palms together), the next might pat hands on knees very quickly, all the way around the circle to the loudest tapping feet faster and faster for a downpour.

2 What other sounds might you build to a roar and then bring back to a purr?

118

LET IT POUR!

- "Rain, rain go away, come again another day." Begin with a downpour. Then eliminate each sound until the person rubbing thumbs against fingers is the only sound left.
- Talk about the different ways rain sounds when falling on a tin roof, on a window, or on the car.

LIGHTNING BOLT!

- You can make raindrops indoors. Ask a grown-up to boil water in a tea kettle. When the steam begins to rise from the kettle, ask the grown-up to hold a tray of ice cubes above the releasing steam. Watch as tiny water droplets collect on the ice tray where the air is cool. When a few droplets combine and fall you've seen a raindrop!

Playing Opossum

When an opossum is frightened or in danger, it "freezes" and doesn't move a muscle. Can you do the same when the music stops?

HERE'S WHAT YOU NEED

Music

Plenty of room to move

HERE'S WHAT YOU DO

1 Have a grown-up turn on the music.

2 Move and dance around the room while the music is playing. When the music stops—FREEZE! Then begin moving again when the music starts.

LET IT POUR!

* Want to make Opossum even more difficult? Stand on one foot when the music stops.

* Here's a way to make cleaning up a game. See how many toys you can put away while the music is playing. When the music stops, you have to stop!

LIGHTNING BOLT!

* Do you know why this game is called Playing Opossum? The opossum is an animal found throughout North America. When it is in danger, first it shows its teeth (it has 50!), then it tries to run away. If another animal catches it, it stays absolutely still as if it were dead. Sometimes the animal chasing it will then lose interest and the opossum will get away.

Bug Hunt

There are many bugs that live outdoors, but do you know how many live indoors, too?

HERE'S WHAT YOU NEED

Hand lens

HERE'S WHAT YOU DO

1 If you were a bug, where would you choose to live inside? Have you ever seen a spider living in a corner? Or a ladybug near a window?

2 Take out your hand lens and go on an indoor bug safari. What types of bugs do you find? Are they all alive? What do you think they eat?

* You won't find any colorful butterflies inside your house, but you many see a moth or two flying around a light bulb. What is the **same** about moths and butterflies, and what is **different**?

* Play Sofa Search. Pull up the couch cushions and see what you find. Put everything in piles, like Dad's stuff, toys, or coins.

* Some bugs are good to have indoors. A few spiders help keep down the bug population. When you find pesky bugs indoors, be sure to use a safe, natural remedy to discourage them. Here's one you can use: If you see lots of ants indoors, bring a cucumber to the rescue! Peel a cucumber with a carrot peeler, place the fresh peels around where you see the ants, and the ants will "hit the road."

123

Ride the Rails

Hop aboard and ride to faraway places on your own imaginary train.

Ticket please!

HERE'S WHAT YOU NEED

Chairs (at least 3)

Poster board or butcher paper

Markers

HERE'S WHAT YOU DO

1   Set up the chairs in a line so that they look like a train.

2   Draw pictures on the poster board or paper to look like views that you might see from a train. Is your train passing through a city or the countryside? Do you see fields with cows or lots of tall buildings and cars? Is the sun out or is it a cloudy day?

3   Place your drawings outside of your train. Make tickets for your passengers. Sit in your train and pretend you are the train engineer, the conductor taking the tickets, a passenger, or bringing up the rear in the caboose.

4   Does your train have a whistle you can blow as you come into the station?

LET IT POUR!

❋   Have you ever gone for a train ride? If you say the words *clickety-clack, clickety-clack,* you will be making the sound of the train's wheels on the track.

❋   How many different ways to travel can you name? Which ones have you taken a ride on and which ones would you like to go on?

❋   If you were taking a train ride in another part of the world, what do you imagine you would see out the window?

❋   Listen to *The Polar Express* by Chris Van Allsburg, about a magical train ride to the North Pole!

No Peeking!

This game is fun no matter where you play it—home, school, or car!

HERE'S WHAT YOU NEED

Pillowcase or bag

Household stuff

Bandanna or scarf (optional)

HERE'S WHAT YOU DO

1 Ask a grown-up to place some things into the pillowcase, like a spoon, ball, apple, doll, toy car, and book.

2 Tie the bandanna around your eyes to blindfold yourself—or close your eyes.

3 Reach into the bag and take out an object. Feel the object carefully. With your eyes covered, can you tell what the object is? Try the game with different objects.

LET IT POUR!

* When you reach in to touch things, let your fingers tell you the shape of each object and how it feels against your skin. Is it **smooth, bumpy,** or **rough**? These are all helpful guessing clues.

* Try using other senses to play the game. Can you identify items by smell? Can you identify the sounds around your house?

LIGHTNING BOLT!

* When you reach into the bag, you are using your sense of touch to help you identify the object. You have five senses in all: touch, taste, smell, sight, hearing. When you use them all, you discover a lot about what is happening around you.

Handy Helpers

Put on an apron or some work clothes and become a handy helper!

HERE'S WHAT YOU NEED

Water and vinegar

Spray bottle

Newspaper

Dust rag or feather duster

HERE'S WHAT YOU DO

1. You can help a lot on a rainy day. Ask a grown-up to spray a mixture of vinegar and water on the low windows. Crumple up an old newspaper and wipe the windows. By the time you are finished the sunlight might be sparkling through!

2 With a feather duster or light dust rag, carefully dust the legs of chairs, desks, tables, and tabletops. In school, perhaps you can clean the board or help stack some books.

I got the paper!

newspaper

LET IT POUR!

* Do you have any regular tasks to do around your house like make your bed, set the table, or hang up your clothes? What do you like to do best?

* What are the Handy Helpers that you can do on a sunny day outdoors?

LIGHTNING BOLT!

* Helping around your house or school can be lots of fun—and you are doing something nice for someone else at the same time. There are lots of things you can do to help people and pets: say "hello" whenever you see them, pick up after yourself, bring the newspaper indoors, make a picture to surprise someone, help put the groceries away, or play with your dog or cat.

Skittleboard

Do you like to play board games? In Skittleboard, you make the board and then have fun playing, too.

HERE'S WHAT YOU NEED

Shirt gift box

Markers or crayons

Ruler

Skittle (button or bottle cap)

Partner

HERE'S WHAT YOU DO

1 Take the shirt box and tear off one of the shorter ends. Use a marker to draw a large U in the box, with the open end of the U at the open end of the box.

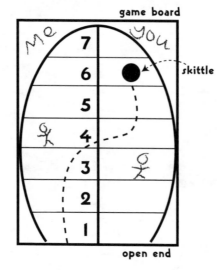

2 Starting at the open end, draw 7 lines across the box. Each line should be about 3 inches (7.5 cm) apart. Draw a line down the center of the game board.

3 Number each of the center sections 1 through 7, starting at the open-ended side. Now your game board is ready!

GAME PLAN!

1 This game is for two players. Each player must pick one side of the board. Take turns gently shooting your skittle from the open end onto the game board. Try to land the skittle in one of the numbered squares.

2 When you land your skittle in a square, without it touching a horizontal line, you then can draw on your side of the square a part of a stick figure person. Begin with a head and continue with each landing in that square until you have completely drawn a stick figure person with two eyes, a nose, mouth, two arms, two feet, and a head.

3 Whoever completes a stick figure in a square first, wins.

SIMPLY SCIENCE

Floating eggs? Raising raisins? Invisible art? Could this be magic? It does seem magical, but actually, it is simply science!

Raising Raisins

How strong are the bubbles in a soft drink? Stronger than you might think!

HERE'S WHAT YOU NEED

Clear drinking glass

Club soda or seltzer

3 raisins

HERE'S WHAT YOU DO

1 Fill the glass with club soda. What do the bubbles in the glass do?

2 Drop the raisins into the glass. Did they sink?

3 Now watch the bubbles and the raisins. What happens to the raisins? Why do you think that happens? What do the bubbles have to do with it?

4 Watch a little longer. What happens next?

LET IT POUR!

✱ Try the same experiment with a maraschino cherry or a raspberry. What happens?

✱ Remove the fruit from the glass. Add some chocolate syrup and a splash of milk. Stir. You made a real New York egg cream! Enjoy.

LIGHTNING BOLT!

✱ The tiny bubbles in soft drinks are filled with gas. This gas is so light that it causes the bubbles to float upward. When raisins are dropped into the drink, the bubbles stick to the raisins. The light gas then carries the raisins to the surface. When the bubbles reach the surface they burst, and the raisins sink.

Clean Coins

When coins are dirty and soap won't do, here's a way to make them look almost new!

HERE'S WHAT YOU NEED

3 dirty pennies

3 clear drinking glasses

Cola

Vinegar

Baking soda

HERE'S WHAT YOU DO

1 Place a dirty penny in each of the glasses.

2 In the first glass, pour enough cola to cover the penny. In the second glass, pour 2 to 3 tablespoons (25–40 ml) of vinegar and about a teaspoon (5 ml) of baking soda. In the last glass, pour enough vinegar to cover the penny.

3 Let the pennies soak for 3 to 4 hours, then fish them out of the glasses with a spoon. Are all the pennies clean? Which penny is the cleanest?

LET IT POUR!

✳ Look at each coin carefully. On one side of the coin you will see the year the penny was made. Which of your pennies is the **oldest**? The **newest**? Do any coins show the year you were born?

✳ Each penny has a **head** and a **tail**. Which side is the head? Toss your penny into the air and guess which side it will land on—heads or tails?

✳ Save your pennies in a jar. When the jar is full, roll them into coin papers; then visit a bank to exchange your pennies for dollars.

LIGHTNING BOLT!

✳ Pennies are used in Great Britain, the United States, Canada, and other countries. In the United States, the penny is also called a cent. You need 100 pennies to equal 1 dollar.

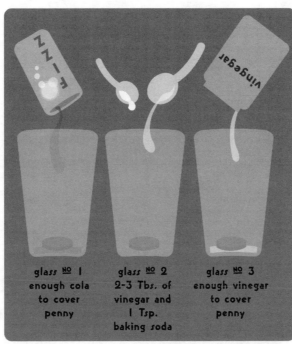

glass № 1
enough cola
to cover
penny

glass № 2
2-3 Tbs. of
vinegar and
1 Tsp.
baking soda

glass № 3
enough vinegar
to cover
penny

Floating Egg

If you have ever been to the ocean, you know that it is easier to float in the ocean's salty water than it is in a freshwater lake. Here is a way that you can see just how saltwater helps things float.

HERE'S WHAT YOU NEED

Water

Egg

Salt

A clear drinking glass

HERE'S WHAT YOU DO

1 Fill the glass halfway with water.

2 Gently lower the egg into the glass. Does it float?

3 Remove the egg carefully. This time, slowly pour salt into the glass of water. What happens to the egg?

LET IT POUR!

* Use a glass filled with salty water and one filled with fresh water. What small items will float in both glasses? What will float only in the salty water? What will not float in either glass?

LIGHTNING BOLT!

* Watch a real stand-up egg. Place a tablespoon (15 ml) of salt on a table. Stand up the egg in the salt. Now, gently blow the salt away. What does the egg do?

* The egg remains standing because there are still a few grains of salt under the egg that are working to hold up the egg.

Bubble Fun

Bubble here and bubble there. Bubbles, bubbles everywhere!

HERE'S WHAT YOU NEED

2 paper clips

Dishwashing liquid

Water

Cup

HERE'S WHAT YOU DO

1 Ask a grown-up to bend one paper clip to form a circle and the other to form a handle.

2 Mix 3 tablespoons of dishwashing liquid into the cup with about a half cup of water.

3 Dip the loop into the mixture and blow steadily through the loop. Watch what happens.

LET IT POUR!

✳ Pour the bubble formula into a shallow dish. Experiment making bubbles with different objects such as the plastic loops from a six-pack of soda, stencils, etc.

✳ Sprinkle dusting powder on the surface of a bowl of water. Add a drop of dishwashing detergent. What happens?

✳ Take a bubble bath!

LIGHTNING BOLT!

✳ Soap bubbles are formed when the dishwashing liquid stretches around tiny pockets of air that are trapped in the running water.

Magic Art

Here is a way to make a secret drawing or send a secret message.

HERE'S WHAT YOU NEED

Cotton swab

Lemon juice

White paper

Iron (for grown-up use only)

HERE'S WHAT YOU DO

1 Dip the cotton swab into the lemon juice and use it to draw a picture on your white paper. Let dry.

2 Ask a grown-up to place a warm iron on the picture. What happens when the heat from the iron is applied to the picture?

LET IT POUR!

❉ Lemon juice is clear, or **invisible**, without the heat. Other colorful berries can be used for drawing, too. Mash some strawberries or blueberries and draw a berry picture using a cotton swab. Can you see it without the iron's heat?

Index

Oceans

A Smithsonian Notable Book

"She delights in looking at the ocean from myriad viewpoints and children will enjoy her multifaceted sensibility." —*School Library Journal*

"Even landlocked students can learn about the ocean and complete the activities in Oceans." —*Curriculum Review*

$14.95 (CAN $22.95) 1-55652-443-9

Rainforests

"A potpourri of resources and activity ideas." —*School Library Journal*

Kids go wild for rainforests! These 50-plus games, activities, and experiments are a jungle of fun whether you live near Olympic National Forest in Washington State or the cornfields of Iowa.

$14.95 (CAN $22.95) 1-55652-476-5

Deserts

"This guide...imparts an impressive amount of information about the subject in a way that appeals to youngsters." —*Science News*

With 50-plus games, activities, and experiments this book offers fun ways to explore all deserts from frozen polar deserts to the sand-based hot and dry deserts. Kids will love learning how animals and plants have adapted to survive in these beautiful but harsh environments.

$14.95 (CAN $22.95) 1-55652-524-9

Available at your favorite bookstore or by calling (800) 888-4741.

Distributed by Independent Publishers Group
www.ipgbook.com

Visit the author's Web site at
www.nancycastaldo.com

CHICAGO REVIEW PRESS